HOW TO DRAW CARTOONS

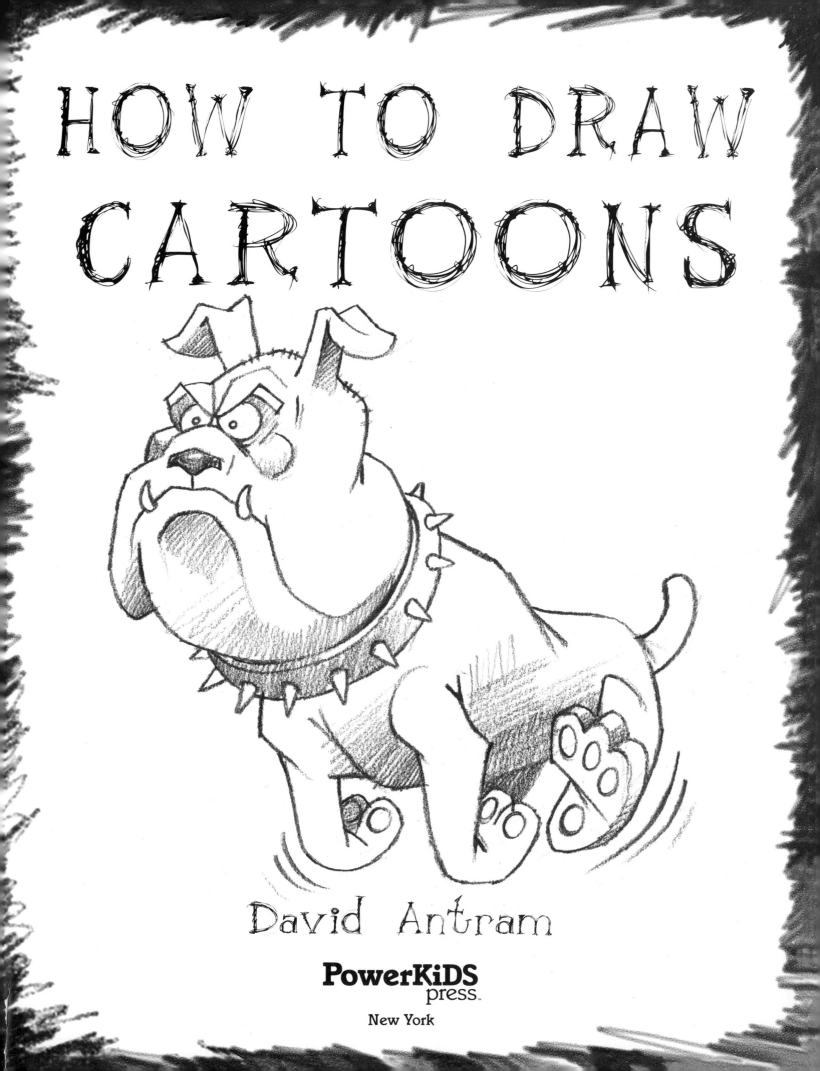

David Antram

PowerKiDS
press™

New York

Published in 2011 by The Rosen Publishing Group, Inc.
29 East 21st Street, New York, NY 10010

Editor: Rob Walker, Stephen Haynes
U.S. Editor: Kara Murray

Library of Congress Cataloging-in-Publication Data

Antram, David.
  How to draw cartoons / David Antram. — 1st ed.
      p. cm.
  Includes index.
   ISBN 978-1-4488-1576-0 (library binding) — ISBN 978-1-4488-1597-5 (pbk.) —
ISBN 978-1-4488-1598-2 (6-pack)
  1. Cartooning—Technique—Juvenile literature. 2. Drawing—Technique—
Juvenile literature. I. Title.
  NC1320.B43 2011
  741.5'1—dc22

2010002563

Manufactured in Heshan, China

CPSIA Compliance Information: Batch #SS0102PK:
For Further Information contact Rosen Publishing, New York,
New York at 1-800-237-9932

Contents

Making a Start

Learning to draw is about looking and seeing. Keep practicing, and get to know your subject. Use a sketchbook to make quick sketches. Start by doodling, and experiment with shapes and patterns. There are many ways to draw, this book shows just one method. Visit art galleries, look at artists' drawings, see how friends draw, but above all, find your own way.

Remember that practice makes perfect. If it looks wrong, start again. Keep working at it. The more you draw, the more you will learn.

Simple shapes for the figure in action

Perspective

If you look at any object from different viewpoints, you will see that the part that is closest to you looks larger, and the part farthest away from you looks smaller. Drawing in perspective is a way of creating a feeling of space, or of showing three dimensions on a flat surface.

It may help you with perspective if you imagine that your figure fits into a rectangular block like this.

The vanishing point (V.P.) is the place in a perspective drawing where parallel lines appear to meet. The position of the vanishing point depends on the viewer's eye level. Sometimes a low viewpoint can give your drawing added drama.

V.P.

Two-point perspective drawing

Two-point perspective uses two vanishing points: one for lines running along the figure, and one on the opposite side for lines running across the figure. This gives a very realistic three-dimensional effect.

Low eye level (view from below)

V.P.

V.P.

Normal eye level

V.P.

V.P.

V.P.

V.P.

High eye level (view from above)

V.P. = vanishing point

7

Drawing Tools

Here are just a few of the many tools that you can use for drawing. Let your imagination go, and have fun experimenting with all the different marks you can make.

Pencil

Watercolour pencil

Charcoal pencil

Charcoal stick

Pastels

Finger painting

Each grade of **pencil** makes a different mark, from fine, gray lines to soft, black ones. Pencils are graded from #1 (the softest) to #4 (the hardest).

Watercolor pencils come in many different colors and make a line similar to a #2 pencil. If you paint over your finished drawing with clean water, though, the lines will soften and run.

It is less messy and easier to achieve a fine line with a **charcoal pencil** than a stick of charcoal. Create soft tones by smudging lines with your finger. **Ask an adult** to spray the drawing with fixative to prevent further smudging.

Pastels are brittle sticks of powdered color. They blend and smudge easily and are ideal for quick sketches. Pastel drawings work well on textured, colored paper. **Ask an adult** to spray your finished drawing with fixative.

Experiment with **finger painting**. Your fingerprints make exciting patterns and textures. Use your fingers to smudge soft pencil, charcoal, and pastel lines.

Black, gray, and white pastel on gray construction paper

Ballpoint pens are very useful for sketching and making notes. Make different tones by building up layers of shading.

A **mapping pen** has to be dipped into bottled ink to fill the nib. Different nib shapes make different marks. Try putting a diluted ink wash over parts of the finished drawing.

Drafting pens and specialist **art pens** can produce extremely fine lines and are ideal for creating surface texture.
A variety of pen nibs are available that produce different widths of line.

Felt—tip pens are ideal for quick sketches. If the ink is not waterproof, try drawing on wet paper and see what happens.

Broad—nibbed **marker pens** make interesting lines and are good for large, bold sketches. Try using a black pen for the main sketch and a gray one to block in areas of shadow.

Paintbrushes are shaped differently to make different marks. Japanese brushes are soft and produce beautiful, flowing lines. Large sable brushes are good for painting a wash over a line drawing. Fine brushes are good for drawing delicate lines.

Ballpoint pen

Mapping pen

Drafting pen

Felt—tip pen

Marker pen

Paintbrush

9

Materials

Try using different types of drawing papers and materials. Experiment with charcoal, wax crayons, and pastels. All pens, from felt—tips to ballpoints, will make interesting marks. Try drawing with pen and ink on wet paper.

Ink silhouette

Felt—tips come in a range of line widths. The wider pens are good for filling in large areas of flat tone.

Pencil drawings can include a vast amount of detail and tone. Try experimenting with the different grades of pencil to get a range of light and shade effects in your drawing.

Remember, the best equipment and materials will not necessarily make the best drawing — only practice will!

Cross—hatching

Hatching

Lines drawn in **ink** cannot be erased, so keep your ink drawings sketchy and not too rigid. Don't worry about mistakes, as these can be lost in the drawing as it develops.

Adding light and shade to a drawing with an ink pen can be tricky. Use solid ink for the very darkest areas and crosshatching (straight lines crisscrossing each other) for ordinary dark tones. Use hatching (straight lines running parallel to each other) for medium tones, and keep the lightest areas empty.

Drawing a Figure

Drawing a cartoon figure can be broken down into stages. Follow the steps shown here. By learning how to build up your drawing in this way, you can create your own cartoons.

Start by sketching these simple shapes.

Head

Draw an oval for the head.

Body

Draw an oval for the body and smaller ovals for the hands.

Hand

Draw an oval for the hips.

Feet

Sketch straight lines for the limbs, adding dots to show the joints.

Now start to build up the basic shape and features of your figure.

Draw a C shape to position the ear. Add straight lines for the exaggerated nose. This head is in profile (side view).

Turn the lines of the arms and legs into simple tube shapes.

Lightly sketch in the shape of the hand and outstretched fingers.

Join the ovals of the body and the hips to get the main shape of the body.

Sketch in simple foot shapes.

Now take your figure a stage further.

Add fingers to the clenched fist.

Using a series of simple lines, add details to the head, defining the shape of the nose, eye, ear, and hair.

Add the slingshot and satchel.

Draw the shape of the hand and its fingers.

Draw the feet and toes.

Draw the legs. You have already marked where the joints are.

Complete the slingshot, adding detail and shading.

Add shading to the head where necessary, and add lines to show the direction of the hair. Finish off the eyes with a dot for the pupil.

Curved lines like these around an object or figure can suggest movement.

Shade areas where light wouldn't reach.

Draw the tunic. Creases in the cloth help show the direction of the arms and legs beneath.

Use shading on the palm of the hand, and add faint lines to show the joints in the fingers.

Complete details of the feet and legs by adding toenails and kneecaps.

Carefully erase any unwanted construction lines that remain.

Heads

Heads come in many shapes and sizes, but this simple set of rules should help you draw any type.

First draw an oval (for a longer head and face, just make the oval longer and thinner).

Now add a narrower oval within the first. This is a construction line to show you where the center line of the face is. The dotted part of this oval represents the back of the head.

Draw a third oval crossing the second one. This is another construction line to help you get the nose and eyes in the right place. Again, the dotted part shows the back of the head.

The point where the second and third ovals cross is the center of the face. Draw in the eyes just above the center.

With these construction lines in place, it is easier to place the facial features and draw the head.

The top of the nose, the middle of the mouth, and the space between the eyes should all line up with the second oval.

You can make the head look in a different direction by changing the width of the inner ovals. This changes the position where the lines cross. This is very useful if you want to draw the same head from different angles.

Making the second oval wider makes the head face more to the side. The cross-over construction lines always help you identify the center of the face.

To draw a head facing down, the second and third ovals should cross in the lower half of the face. Use the construction lines each time to position the facial features. See how the mouth is mostly hidden by the nose.

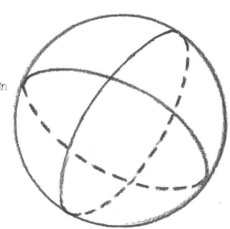

To make the head look up, the second and third ovals must cross in the upper half of the face. Again use the construction lines to draw in the features. See how much space the mouth takes up in this view.

15

Expressions

Drawing different expressions is very important in cartoons. It's the best way to show what your character is thinking or feeling. Try drawing many different facial expressions. Don't be afraid to exaggerate them for comic effect.

Start by drawing an oval shape.

Head

Arched eyebrows

Sketch the other two ovals as you did before (pages 14—15).

Angular mouth

Using your construction lines as before, add the basic details of the face. This character looks angry.

Using a Mirror
Look at your own face in the mirror. By making different expressions, you will see how to draw these in your cartoons.

Gritted teeth

Finish the drawing by adding eyes, teeth, and hair. Shade in the areas you want to be darker.

Now try drawing some different expressions. Here are a few ideas to get you started.

Giggling

Laughing

Frightened

Tired

Smiling

Puzzled

Characters

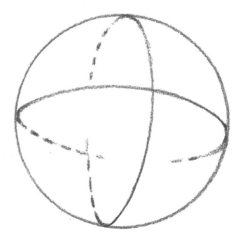

Creating different characters is fun and will expand your cartoon—drawing skills. Try to make each character different from the last. Give each one distinctive features to show their different personalities.

Start by drawing the oval construction lines for a head.

Roughly sketch the facial features. For this character, draw the eyes quite small and close together.

Adding a hat can make a character look quite different from the others.

Make the mouth small, too.

This character's chin has been exaggerated. By drawing beyond the construction lines, you can exaggerate any feature.

Start each character using the oval construction lines for the head.

This character's defining features are a long, narrow head, a large nose, and a wide mouth.

This character has arched eyebrows and a wide grin.

The wide mouth has been exaggerated beyond the construction lines. This makes him look grumpy.

The eyes make this one look sneaky.

This character has high eyebrows, a narrow head, and a small mouth, which all make him look a bit foolish.

This character's main features are his large, beaklike nose and drooping mustache.

The narrowed eyes and crafty smile make the character look quite villainous.

19

Figure Work

Adding clothes to a figure can help define the character. This figure is dressed as a Victorian maid.

Start by sketching these simple shapes for the figure.

Draw an oval for the hand.

Add ovals for the body and hips.

Sketch an oval for the head.

Head

Body

Draw straight lines to connect the ovals and show the positions of the limbs.

Hips

Indicate the joints with dots.

Legs

Draw two shapes for the feet.

Feet

Position the facial features as before.

Inside the hand shape, draw a circle and one finger going into the mouth.

Draw tube shapes for the arms, using your construction lines as a guide.

Join the body and hips into one large oval.

Make the legs into tube shapes.

Add a small circle for the position of the big toe. This will help you draw the shoes.

Drawing Hands

1 2 3 4

Follow these steps to help you draw the shape of a hand. As you get better, you will be able to draw different hand gestures.

20

Add more facial features and draw in the shape of the face, using the construction lines as a guide.

Sketch the hair and add the cap.

Finish the head by adding the hair and eyelashes. Shade above the eyes and inside the ear.

Draw the shape of the clothes going around the body.

Sketch the dress using curved lines.

Dress

Add details such as cuffs, buttons, and a collar.

Add lines to the apron and at the bottom of the dress to show folds in the material.

The hem of the dress covers part of the feet.

Two parallel lines show the soles of the shoes.

Try drawing these hand gestures.

Add shading to areas like this where light wouldn't reach.

Remove any unwanted construction lines.

21

Figure in Costume

This cartoon character is an Inca warrior. With his costume and weapons, he is a very distinctive figure.

A straight line with an oval on top shows the position of the club.

Head

Sketch the main shapes of the figure.

Club

Sketch the features of the face. Use the construction lines to help place the eyes, nose, and mouth.

Use ovals for the head, body, hands, and hips.

Add a straight line for the staff.

Body

Hips

Indicate the joints with dots.

Legs

Start to sketch in the shape of the hand.

Feet

Make the body and hips into one large oval.

Draw tube-shaped arms and legs. Remember, the dots show where the joints are.

Draw curved shapes for the position of the feet.

The headdress is made up of diamond shapes. Sketch these along the top of the head.

Extend the shape of the face beyond the construction lines and add more detail to the eyes.

Each of the diamond shapes needs a line down the center to make it look like a feather.

Sketch curved lines to draw the club.

Draw the fingers.

Draw a large circle for the medallion.

Add more detail to the face.

Start sketching in clothes using simple shapes.

A few wavy lines make the medallion look reflective.

Draw lines on the club to make it woodlike.

Add toes and sandals to the feet.

Shade alternate squares on the warrior's tunic.

Shade areas like this where light wouldn't reach.

Add lines to show costume detail.

Complete the details of the feet and sandals.

Remove any unwanted construction lines.

23

Monster

This cartoon monster has just been awakened by a massive bolt of lightning. Adding backgrounds and effects like these can bring your drawing to life, too!

Start by sketching in the shape of the figure as it sits bolt upright.

Sketch in simple shapes for the hands and thumbs.

Head

Body

Arm

Hand

This monster has no neck, so overlap the oval of the head with the oval for the body.

Add straight lines for the arms and legs with dots to indicate the joints.

Draw a line to show the position of the bench.

Draw a curved line to make a flat top for the monster's head.

Add some basic facial features using circles for the eyes and the nose.

Sketch tube—shaped arms and legs, adding a circle for each knee.

Sketch the shape of the monster's feet, adding a big toe, too.

Sharp, spiky lines coming from the monster show the bolt of electricity.

Add detail to the face. Shading above the eyes makes the brow jut forward.

Draw the monster's sleeves with his arms poking out to exaggerate his size.

Sketch fingers.

Add the rest of the toes and draw in toenails.

Draw a belt around the monster's waist.

Draw more lines to create the bench.

Finish the detail on the head.

Shading makes the lightning bolt look brighter.

Add stitches to the monster's wrists and forehead.

Finish the details of the hands, adding fingernails and knuckles.

Add shading and creases to the monster's clothes.

Finish drawing the bench.

Remove any unwanted construction lines.

25

Rats

Animals like rats make great cartoon characters. You can give them personalities and expressions, just as you can with your cartoon people.

Start your drawing by sketching in simple shapes.

Head

Body

Tail

Feet

Sketch an oval for the head, with a line for the top of the nose.

Sketch a small oval for the top of the body, then a larger one for the lower part of the body.

Add a line for the tail.

Use lines for the limbs, with dots to indicate joints.

Sketch the neck and arms using simple tube shapes.

Add the main features to the rat's head, using simple shapes for the ears and eyes.

Add another line to the tail.

The rat's nose is made up of a circle and two lines to join it to the head. Use the line you made earlier to help position it.

Sketch the legs and feet using your first construction lines as a guide.

Use simple, curved lines to show the inner part of the ear.

Sketch more detail on the rat's head.

Add fingers to the paws.

Remember to give your rats expressions, just like you would with humans! The positioning of the eye makes one rat look sneaky, but the other looks unsure.

Sketch a line for the end of the tail.

Draw a small circle to show the rat's ankle bone.

Add toes to the rat's long rear paws.

Add tone to the drawing to give it more impact.

Use short, spiky lines for the rat's fur.

Chiaroscuro
The use of light and dark to create bold, dramatic images is called chiaroscuro. Try this on your cartoon.

Make the edges of the body jagged to show the fur.

Add shading to the areas that face away from the light.

Draw lines across the rat's tail to complete it.

Remove any unwanted construction lines.

27

Bulldog

The bulldog is a classic cartoon character. Its face is perfect for a grumpy expression, which instantly gives it a character all its own.

Mark the positions of the ears and the nose.

The main shape of the bulldog is made with different-sized overlapping circles.

Draw a short line for the tail.

Body

Legs

Add short, curved lines for the legs.

Draw the shape of the ears.

Add circles for the eyes, with straight lines above to make them look more aggressive.

Using the construction lines as a guide, add in the mouth and jowls.

Join the two circles of the body with straight lines.

Sketch two curved lines for the neck and collar.

Add the front legs and paws.

This foot is upturned, so you see only the sole. Sketch this in as a simple shape.

Add detail to the face.

Draw the shape of the bulldog's back.

Draw more detail on the mouth and nose.

Finish the tail with curved lines.

Add small cones for the spikes on the collar.

Add areas of shade on the nose and around the eyes.

Add toes to the dog's paws.

Draw the final details of the head.

Shade areas around the collar and jowls.

Curved lines beside the legs give a feeling of movement.

Add shading to the underside of the bulldog.

Remove any unwanted construction lines.

Finish the paw of the bulldog with small circles.

29

Man on a Donkey

Drawing a person sitting or riding on an animal is another useful skill to master when drawing cartoons. This character is riding a donkey.

Head

First draw in the main shapes of the figure and the donkey.

Arm

Hand

Ears

Draw ovals for the main body areas and straight lines for the limbs.

Leg

Hooves

Sketch the basic facial features.

Sketch the donkey's neck.

Draw simple shapes for the hooves.

Draw tube shapes for each of the limbs.

Add curved lines to complete the shape of the donkey's body.

Add a tuft of hair between the donkey's ears.

Sketch the position of the donkey's downturned eyelids.

Draw the donkey's legs, with circles for knee and ankle joints.

Add the shape of the man's feet.

Draw a circle for the nostrils.

Add clothes to the man.

Add hair and more facial features.

Sketch fingers.

Add lines to show the inside of the donkey's ears.

Draw the reins and bridle.

Finish the detail on the head, shading under the chin and around the neck.

Draw the shape of the donkey's legs in more detail.

Add toes to the man's feet.

Complete the detail of the hands.

Shade the back of the donkey's ear.

Add lines for creases in the robe's material.

Composition
Framing your drawing with a square or rectangle can make it look completely different.

Add final details to the man's feet and to the donkey's hooves.

Shade areas where light would not reach.

Remove any unwanted construction lines.

31

Glossary

chiaroscuro (kee–ahr––uh–SKYUHR–oh) The use of light and dark in a drawing.

composition (kom–puh–ZIH–shun) The positioning of a picture on the drawing paper.

construction lines (kun–STRUK–shun LYNZ) Guidelines used in the early stages of a drawing and usually erased later.

crosshatching (KRAWS–hach–ing) A series of crisscrossing lines used to add shade to a drawing.

fixative (FIK–suh–tiv) A type of resin used to spray over a finished drawing to prevent smudging. **It should be used only by an adult.**

hatching (HACH–ing) A series of parallel lines used to add shade to a drawing.

profile (PROH–fyl) A view from the side, especially a side view of a person's head or face.

silhouette (sih–luh–WET) A drawing that shows only a dark shape, like a shadow.

sketchbook (SKECH–buhk) A book for making quick drawings.

three–dimensional (three–deh–MENCH–nul) Having an effect of depth, so as to look lifelike or real.

vanishing point (VA–nish–ing POYNT) The place in a perspective drawing where parallel lines appear to meet.

Index

Web Sites

Due to the changing nature of Internet links, PowerKids Press has developed an online list of Web sites related to the subject of this book. This site is updated regularly. Please use this link to access the list:

www.powerkidslinks.com/howtodraw/cartoons/